The Wiersbe
BIBLE STUDY SERIES

The Wiersbe
BIBLE STUDY SERIES

HEBREWS

Live by

Faith, Not

by Sight

DAVID C COOK

transforming lives together

THE WIERSBE BIBLE STUDY SERIES: HEBREWS
Published by David C Cook
4050 Lee Vance Drive
Colorado Springs, CO 80918 U.S.A.

Integrity Music Limited, a Division of David C Cook
Brighton, East Sussex BN1 2RE, England

The graphic circle C logo is a registered trademark of David C Cook.

ISBN 978-0-7814-4566-5
eISBN 978-0-7814-0629-1

The Team: Steve Parolini, Karen Lee-Thorp,
Amy Kiechlin, Jack Campbell, and Susan Vannaman
Series Cover Design: John Hamilton Design
Cover Photo: Veer Inc., Alloy Photography

Printed in the United States of America

First Edition 2009

12 13 14 15 16 17 18 19 20 21

111521

Contents

Introduction to Hebrews

A Much-Needed Shake-Up

The epistle of Hebrews was written at a time when the ages were colliding and when everything in society seemed to be shaking. It was written to Christians who were wondering what was going on and what they could do about it.

One of the major themes of Hebrews is: Be confident! God is shaking things up so that you may learn to live by faith and not by sight.

Three Important Words

The word *better* is used thirteen times in the book of Hebrews as the writer shows the superiority of Christ and His salvation over the Hebrew system of religion. Another word that is repeated in this book is *perfect;* in the original Greek it is used fourteen times. It means a perfect standing before God. *Eternal* is a third word that is important to the message of Hebrews. When you combine these three words, you discover that Jesus Christ and the Christian life He gives us are better because these blessings are eternal and they give us perfect standing before God.

Faith for Tough Times

So why did the writer of Hebrews ask his readers to evaluate their faith? Because they were going through difficult times and were being tempted to go back to the Jewish religion. The temple was still standing when this book was written and all the priestly ceremonies were still being carried on daily.

These people were "second-generation believers," having been won to Christ by those who had known Jesus during His ministry on earth. They were true believers who had been persecuted because of their faith. But they were being seduced by teachers of false doctrine and were in danger of forgetting the true Word that their first leaders, now dead, had taught them.

Hebrews is a book of evaluation, proving that Jesus Christ is better than anything the law of Moses has to offer.

Looking Ahead

The focus in Hebrews is ultimately on the future. The writer informs us that he is speaking about "the world to come," a time when believers will reign with Christ. You and I as God's children have been promised a future reward. As with Abraham and Moses of old, the decisions we make today will determine the rewards tomorrow. Dr. A. W. Tozer used to remind us, "Every man must choose his world." True believers have "tasted the good word of God, and the powers of the world [age] to come" (Heb. 6:5 KJV); this should mean we have no interest in or appetite for the present sinful world system.

Our Purpose

Hebrews is a book packed with theology. But as we study this letter, we must keep in mind that our purpose is not to get lost in curious doctrinal details. Nor is our purpose to attack or defend some pet doctrine. Our purpose is to hear God speak in Jesus Christ, and to heed that Word. If our purpose is to know Christ better and exalt Him more, then whatever differences we may have in our understanding of the book will be forgotten in our worship of Him.

—*Warren W. Wiersbe*

How to Use This Study

This study is designed for both individual and small-group use. We've divided it into ten lessons—each references one or more chapters in Warren W. Wiersbe's commentary *Be Confident* (second edition, David C. Cook, 2009). While reading *Be Confident* is not a prerequisite for going through this study, the additional insights and background Wiersbe offers can greatly enhance your study experience.

The Getting Started questions at the beginning of each lesson offer you an opportunity to record your first thoughts and reactions to the study text. This is an important step in the study process as those "first impressions" often include clues about what it is your heart is longing to discover.

The bulk of the study is found in the Going Deeper questions. These dive into the Bible text and, along with excerpts from Wiersbe's commentary, help you examine not only the original context and meaning of the verses but also modern application.

Looking Inward narrows the focus down to your personal story. These intimate questions can be uncomfortable at times, but don't shy away from honesty here. This is where you are asked to stand before the mirror of God's Word and look closely at what you see. It's the place to take a good look at yourself in light of the lesson and search for ways in which you can grow in faith.

Going Forward is the place where you can commit to paper those things you want or need to do in order to better live out the discoveries you made in the Looking Inward section. Don't skip or skim through this. Take the time to really consider what practical steps you might take to move closer to Christ. Then share your thoughts with a trusted friend who can act as an encourager and accountability partner.

Finally, there is a brief Seeking Help section to close the lesson. This is a reminder for you to invite God into your spiritual-growth process. If you choose to write out a prayer in this section, come back to it as you work through the lesson and continue to seek the Holy Spirit's guidance as you discover God's will for your life.

Tips for Small Groups

A small group is a dynamic thing. One week it might seem like a group of close-knit friends. The next it might seem more like a group of uncomfortable strangers. A small-group leader's role is to read these subtle changes and adjust the tone of the discussion accordingly.

Small groups need to be safe places for people to talk openly. Through shared wrestling with difficult life issues, some of the greatest personal growth takes off. But in order for the group to feel safe, participants need to know it's okay *not* to share sometimes. Always invite honest disclosure, but never force someone to speak if he or she isn't comfortable doing so. (A savvy leader will follow up later with a group member who isn't comfortable sharing in a group setting to see if a one-on-one discussion is more appropriate.)

Have volunteers take turns reading excerpts from Scripture or from the commentary. The more each person is involved, even in the mundane tasks, the more they'll feel comfortable opening up in more meaningful ways.

The leader should watch the clock and keep the discussion moving. Sometimes there may be more Going Deeper questions than your group can cover in your available time. If you've had a fruitful discussion, it's okay to move on without finishing everything. And if you think the group is getting bogged down on a question or has taken off on a tangent, you can simply say, "Let's go on to question 5." Be sure to save at least ten or fifteen minutes for the Going Forward questions.

Finally, soak your group meetings in prayer—before you begin, during as needed, and always at the end of your time together.

Above the Angels

(HEBREWS 1:1—2:18)

Before you begin ...
- *Pray for the Holy Spirit to reveal truth and wisdom as you go through this lesson.*
- *Read Hebrews 1:1—2:18. This lesson references chapters 1 and 2 in* Be Confident. *It will be helpful for you to have your Bible and a copy of the commentary available as you work through this lesson.*

Getting Started

From the Commentary

Many people have avoided the epistle to the Hebrews and, consequently, have robbed themselves of practical spiritual help. Some have avoided this book because they are afraid of it. The "warnings" in Hebrews have made them uneasy. Others have avoided this book because they think it is "too difficult" for the average Bible student. To be sure, there are some profound truths in Hebrews, and no preacher or teacher would dare to claim that he knows them all! But the general message of the book is clear and there is no reason why you and I should not understand and profit from it.

—*Be Confident*, pages 17–18

1. What is your initial response to what you've read in Hebrews so far? In what ways, if any, do you relate to the fears Wiersbe references? What is the value of digging into the more difficult Scripture passages?

More to Consider: This chapter is about how Christ is greater than angels. Read about the importance of angels in Deuteronomy 33:2; Psalm 68:17; Acts 7:53; and Galatians 3:19. Based on what you read, why do you think it is important for the writer of Hebrews to empha-size Jesus' superiority over angels?

2. Choose one verse or phrase from Hebrews 1:1—2:18 that stands out to you. This could be something you're intrigued by, something that makes you uncomfortable, something that puzzles you, something that resonates with you, or just something you want to examine further. Write that here. What strikes you about this verse?

Going Deeper

From the Commentary

> The "more excellent name" that Jesus possesses is "Son."
> While the angels *collectively* may be termed "the sons of
> God" (Job 1:6), no angel would be given this title *individ-
> ually*. It belongs uniquely to our Lord Jesus Christ.
>
> —*Be Confident,* page 32

3. How does the description of Jesus in 1:4–5 set the basis for the rest of this
letter? Why is it critical to the author of Hebrews to differentiate between
the "sons of God" and "God's Son"?

From the Commentary

> [Hebrews 2:1–4] is the first of the five admonitions found
> in Hebrews. Their purpose is to encourage all readers to
> pay attention to God's Word and obey it. We have already
> noted that these admonitions become stronger as we prog-
> ress through the book, from *drifting* from God's Word to
> *defying* God's Word (Heb. 12:14–29).

The [first admonition: Heed the Word and don't drift] is written to believers, for the writer included himself when he wrote "we." The danger here is that of *neglecting our salvation.*

—*Be Confident,* page 34

4. What does it look like to "drift" from salvation? How does neglecting salvation differ from rejecting salvation? What are the dangers of neglecting salvation?

From Today's World

Although the label "political correctness" may have lost some of its impact on our world, the tendency to "speak carefully" about issues that might be sensitive to one group or another remains a constant in our culture. Sometimes, the same sort of "softening of the words" sneaks into churches, effectively giving less prominence to God's Word and more to behavioral issues that make sermons sound more like self-help pep talks than biblically focused teaching. This is also evident in the publishing world, where books on "how to be the best person you can be" litter the shelves of Christian bookstores.

5. The author of Hebrews is concerned about people drifting from God's Word. How does a self-improvement approach to church lead to drifting? What are other ways that our culture encourages "drift" instead of

pursuit of God's truth? What are some safeguards that a church can put into place to assure there is little or no drift in its approach to teaching?

From the Commentary

> When God created the first man and woman, He gave them dominion over His creation (Gen. 1:26–31). David marveled that God would share His power and glory with feeble man! Man was created "a little lower than the angels" (and therefore inferior to them), but man was given privileges far higher than the angels. God never promised the angels that they would reign in "the world to come" (Heb. 2:5).
>
> —*Be Confident,* page 37

6. What surprises do you uncover about God and angels in 1:5–14 and 2:5–9? If man is a "little lower than the angels," why then would God choose humanity to reign with Him in the world to come? What does this say about God's creation of man and woman?

From the Commentary

> Christ is united to us, and we are united to Him: We are
> spiritually one. In fact, we are His "brethren" (Heb. 2:12).
> The writer quoted Psalm 22:22—a messianic psalm—in
> which Christ refers to His church as His brethren. This
> means we and the Son of God share the same nature and
> belong to the same family!
>
> —*Be Confident,* page 38

7. What are the implications of being Christ's "brethren"? For exam-
ple, how does that affect the way Christians view their relationship with
God? With one another? What does it say about the importance of being
"Christlike"?

From the Commentary

> Angels cannot die. Jesus did not come to save angels (note
> Heb. 2:16); He came to save humans. This meant that
> He had to take on Himself flesh and blood and become
> a man. Only then could He die and through His death
> defeat Satan. The word *destroy* does not mean "annihilate,"

for it is obvious that Satan is still alive and busy. The word means "render inoperative, make of none effect." Satan is not destroyed, but he is disarmed.

—*Be Confident,* page 39

8. In everyday terms, what does it mean that Satan is disarmed (2:14–16)? How has Jesus disarmed Satan (2:9, 17–18)?

More to Consider: Hebrews teaches that Jesus' humanity enabled Him to be a sympathetic High Priest to His people (2:17–18). Compare this to an example of an unsympathetic high priest, Eli, as recorded in 1 Samuel 1:9–18.

From the Commentary

Jesus Christ is both merciful and faithful: He is merciful toward people and faithful toward God. He can never fail in His priestly ministries. He made the necessary sacrifice for our sins so that we might be reconciled to God.

He did not need to make a sacrifice for Himself, because He is sinless.

—*Be Confident,* page 40

9. How is Jesus' mercy revealed in the lives of believers? What are some specific examples of His faithfulness toward God? Why are these equally crucial elements in understanding Jesus' role in God's greater plan?

From the Commentary

It might be good at this point to explain the difference between our Lord's ministry as High Priest and His ministry as Advocate (1 John 2:1). As our High Priest, our Lord is able to give us grace to keep us from sinning when we are tempted. If we do sin, then He as our Advocate represents us before the throne of God and forgives us when we sincerely confess our sins to Him (1 John 1:5—2:2). Both of these ministries are involved in His present work of intercession, and it is this intercessory ministry that is the guarantee of our eternal salvation (note that in Heb. 7:25 it is "*to* the uttermost"—i.e., eternally—and not "*from* the uttermost").

—*Be Confident,* pages 40–41

10. Describe the difference between Christ's two roles in your own words. How do we, as Christians, interact with Christ as High Priest? How do we interact with Him as Advocate? How does doing this build our confidence?

Looking Inward

Take a moment to reflect on all that you've explored thus far in this study of Hebrews 1:1—2:18. Review your notes and answers and think about how each of these things matters in your life today.

Tips for Small Groups: To get the most out of this section, form pairs or trios and have group members take turns answering these questions. Be honest and as open as you can in this discussion, but most of all, be encouraging and supportive of others. Be sensitive to those who are going through particularly difficult times and don't press people to speak if they're uncomfortable doing so.

11. How does it make you feel to know that even though you were created "a little lower than the angels," God has chosen you to reign with Him in the new world? How does this affect your view of angels?

12. Have you "drifted" from salvation or from God's Word? If so, how? What prompted these "drifts"? What are practical ways to anchor yourself to God's Word so you are able to avoid drifting?

13. How have you seen Jesus' mercy revealed in your life? In what ways have you experienced the truth that Satan is disarmed? If you have doubted either of these, why?

Going Forward

14. Think of one or two things you have learned from this lesson that you'd like to incorporate into your life more fully in the coming week. Remember that this is all about quality, not quantity. It's better to work on one specific area of life and do it well than to aim at many and do poorly (or to be so overwhelmed that you simply don't try).

Do you need to work on anchoring your faith to God's Word? Study and reflect on Jesus' role as High Priest. Be specific. Go back through Hebrews 1:1—2:18 and put a star next to the phrase or verse that is most encouraging to you. Consider memorizing this verse.

Real-Life Application Ideas: Sometimes we study a passage of the Bible and then move on with our lives, and by the next day or week we don't remember what the passage said, and we drift from it. By rereading the same sentence or paragraph for several days and thinking about it when we're in the car or in the shower, we can move it into our hearts where it affects our behavior. For example, as you're driving to work, you could have a mental conversation with your High Priest, who has disarmed Satan and offers you the strength to resist the temptation to resent a particular coworker.

Seeking Help

15. Write a prayer below (or simply pray one in silence), inviting God to work on your mind and heart in those areas you've previously noted. Be honest about your desires and fears.

Notes for Small Groups:

- *Look for ways to put into practice the things you wrote in the Going Forward section. Talk with other group members about your ideas and commit to being accountable to one another.*

- *During the coming week, ask the Holy Spirit to continue to reveal truth to you from what you've read and studied.*

- *Before you start the next lesson, read Hebrews 3:1— 4:13. For more in-depth lesson preparation, read chapter 3, "Greater Than Moses," in* Be Confident.

More Than Moses

(HEBREWS 3:1—4:13)

Before you begin …
- *Pray for the Holy Spirit to reveal truth and wisdom as you go through this lesson.*
- *Read Hebrews 3:1—4:13. This lesson references chapter 3 in* Be Confident. *It will be helpful for you to have your Bible and a copy of the commentary available as you work through this lesson.*

Getting Started

From the Commentary

Next to Abraham, Moses was undoubtedly the man most greatly revered by the Jewish people. To go back to the law meant to go back to Moses, and the recipients of this letter to the Hebrews were sorely tempted to do just that. It was important that the writer convince his readers that Jesus Christ is greater than Moses, for the entire system of Jewish religion came through Moses. In this section, we learn that Jesus Christ is superior to Moses.

—Be Confident, *page 45*

1. The original readers of Hebrews had probably been raised as Jews, living by the law of Moses. When they became Christians, their Jewish family members were understandably horrified, and their pagan neighbors thought they were idiots. They may have lost the network of family, friends, and business contacts they had as observant Jews. They weren't getting arrested for being Christian, but they were being insulted and excluded. All that would stop if they simply abandoned Christian practices and went back to living like observant Jews.

What price do some Christians today have to pay for living as Christians? What might make a Christian today wonder whether Christ is really superior to the available alternatives?

More to Consider: The author of Hebrews focuses his message on believers. Why is that significant to his message?

2. Choose one verse or phrase from Hebrews 3:1—4:13 that stands out to you. This could be something you're intrigued by, something that makes you uncomfortable, something that puzzles you, something that resonates with you, or just something you want to examine further. Write that here. What strikes you about this verse?

Going Deeper

From the Commentary

True Christians not only share in a heavenly calling, but they also share in Jesus Christ (Heb. 3:14). Through the Holy Spirit, we are "members of his body, of his flesh, and of his bones" (Eph. 5:30). True believers are also "partakers of the Holy Ghost" (Heb. 6:4). "Now if any man have not the Spirit of Christ, he is none of his" (Rom. 8:9). Because we are God's children, we also partake in God's loving chastening (Heb. 12:8). Not to be chastened is evidence that a person is not one of God's children.

—*Be Confident,* pages 45–46

3. Why does the author of Hebrews make the point that Jesus has been found worthy of greater honor than Moses? What evidence do you find in 3:1–6 that Jesus is superior to Moses? Can you think of any other evidence? If so, what is it?

From the Commentary

> That Christ is superior to Moses in His person is an obvi-
> ous fact. Moses was a mere man, called to be a prophet
> and leader, while Jesus Christ is the Son of God sent by
> the Father into the world. The title *apostle* means "one sent
> with a commission." Moses was called and commissioned
> by God, but Jesus Christ was *sent* as God's "last Word" to
> sinful man.
>
> —*Be Confident,* page 46

4. What is significant about this distinction between being "sent with a
commission" and being "sent as God's 'last Word'"? (Read John 3:17, 34;
5:36, 38; 6:29, 57; 7:29; 8:42; 10:36; 11:42; and 17:3 for more about Jesus
being sent from God.)

From Today's World

It's not uncommon for people of an older generation to pine for the "good
old days" when confronted with something new. This longing to go back
to the way things were can be prompted by fear of change, or a preference
for familiar comfort over having to learn something new. Our culture expe-
riences this, but nothing to the degree that people in the first century AD

did. Today, many people assume that new is always better and cooler, while old equals outmoded. But in the first century, almost everybody mistrusted anything new.

5. Why is it easy for some people to long for the "good old days" instead of seeking to understand new things?

Ironically, today Christians are likely to falter in their faithfulness not because Christianity is an innovation, but because it's old. Why do some people see Christian faith as old-fashioned? What does 3:7–14 say to those who have doubts about Christ either because He's new or because He's old?

From the Commentary

The word *confidence* literally means "freedom of speech, openness." When you are free to speak, then there is no fear and you have confidence. A believer can come with boldness (synonym of *confidence*) to the throne of grace (Heb. 4:16) with openness and freedom and not be afraid. We have this boldness because of the shed blood of Jesus Christ (Heb. 10:19). Therefore, we should not cast away our confidence, no matter what the circumstances might be.

—*Be Confident,* page 48

6. Circle the things the author of Hebrews says in 3:1—4:13 that are meant to instill confidence in his readers. Why is confidence such a huge theme in this section? How does confidence in Christ's role affect the manner in which believers live? In how they reach out to nonbelievers?

From the Commentary

The wandering of Israel in the wilderness is a major topic in this section. Two men in that nation—Caleb and Joshua—illustrate the attitude described in Hebrews 3:6. Everybody else in Israel over the age of twenty was to die in the wilderness and never enter the Promised Land (see Num. 14:26–38). But Caleb and Joshua believed God, and God honored their faith.

—*Be Confident,* page 49

7. What is the attitude described in Hebrews 3:6? Why didn't the rest of the Israelites have this attitude? What was the blessing given to those who had confidence in God? How does this apply to our confidence in Christ today?

From the Commentary

> The heart of every problem is a problem in the heart.
>
> *—Be Confident,* page 52

8. What does "a problem in the heart" mean? How is this truth evident in Hebrews? Where do you see this in today's church?

More to Consider: Discuss what it means to have a "hard heart." What leads to a hard heart? What are the dangers of developing a hard heart?

From the Commentary

> The emphasis in Hebrews is that true believers have an eternal salvation because they trust a living Savior who constantly intercedes for them. But the writer was careful to point out that this confidence is no excuse for sin.
>
> *—Be Confident,* page 54

9. How might confidence in Jesus lead to sin? What are examples of this in today's church? According to the author of Hebrews, what does it take to not "fall short" of entering "God's rest"?

From the Commentary

> Before Joshua conquered Jericho, he went out to survey the situation, and he met the Lord Jesus Christ (Josh. 5:13–15). Joshua discovered that he was second in command! The Lord had a sword in His hand, and Joshua fell at His feet in complete submission. It was this action in private that gave Joshua his public victory.
>
> We, too, claim our spiritual inheritance by surrendering to Him and trusting His Word.
>
> —*Be Confident,* page 56

10. What are the private actions that give Christians their strength today?

11. According to Hebrews 4:13, "nothing in all creation is hidden from God's sight." How should that motivate us to think and behave?

Looking Inward

Take a moment to reflect on all that you've explored thus far in this study of Hebrews 3:1—4:13. Review your notes and answers and think about how each of these things matters in your life today.

Tips for Small Groups: To get the most out of this section, form pairs or trios and have group members take turns answering these questions. Be honest and as open as you can in this discussion, but most of all, be encouraging and supportive of others. Be sensitive to those who are going through particularly difficult times and don't press people to speak if they're uncomfortable doing so.

12. When have you been tempted to go back to the way things were when you should have pressed forward? Why did that seem appealing to you? When have you been tempted to move on to something new when you should have held fast? Why did that seem appealing to you?

13. What gives you confidence in Jesus? What challenges that confidence? Is "confidence" in Christ the same as "certainty"? Where does doubt fit into your experience of faith?

14. Have you ever used confidence in God as an excuse for sin? If so, what prompted this way of thinking? Instead of a "license to sin," what are some ways you can view the consequences of confidence in Christ?

Going Forward

15. Think of one or two things that you have learned that you'd like to work on in the coming week. Remember that this is all about quality, not quantity. It's better to work on one specific area of life and do it well than to work on many and do poorly (or to be so overwhelmed that you simply don't try).

Do you need to grow in your confidence? Do you need to avoid excusing sin because of your confidence in Christ? Be specific. Go back through Hebrews 3:1—4:13 and put a star next to the phrase or verse that is most encouraging to you. Consider memorizing this verse.

Real-Life Application Ideas: Consider the things you're uncertain about in your life—job, family, church, anything at all. In what ways is your attitude toward these things like or unlike that of Caleb and Joshua? What are some practical things you should be doing to grow in confidence that God is going to lead you in the right direction in each of these areas of life? Do you need to spend more time in prayer? Listen to the wise counsel of others? Make a plan to do these things.

Seeking Help

16. Write a prayer below (or simply pray one in silence), inviting God to work on your mind and heart in those areas you've previously noted. Be honest about your desires and fears.

Notes for Small Groups:

- *Look for ways to put into practice the things you wrote in the Going Forward section. Talk with other group members about your ideas and commit to being accountable to one another.*

- *During the coming week, ask the Holy Spirit to continue to reveal truth to you from what you've read and studied.*

- *Before you start the next lesson, read Hebrews 4:14—5:10. For more in-depth lesson preparation, read chapter 4, "Greater Than Aaron the High Priest,"* in Be Confident.

The True High Priest
(HEBREWS 4:14—5:10)

Before you begin ...

- *Pray for the Holy Spirit to reveal truth and wisdom as you go through this lesson.*
- *Read Hebrews 4:14—5:10. This lesson references chapter 4 in* Be Confident. *It will be helpful for you to have your Bible and a copy of the commentary available as you work through this lesson.*

Getting Started

From the Commentary

The Hebrew Christians who received this letter were sorely tempted to return to the religion of their fathers. After all, any Jew could travel to Jerusalem and *see* the temple and the priests ministering at the altar. Here was something real, visible, concrete. When a person is going through persecution, as these Hebrew Christians were, it is much easier to walk by sight than by faith.

—Be Confident, page 59

1. Why does persecution make it more difficult to walk by faith? What are some of the provocations today's Christians face that make them doubt God?

More to Consider: Before going any further, what would you say are the main arguments to prove the author's assertions that Jesus' role as High Priest is superior to Aaron's?

2. Choose one verse or phrase from Hebrews 4:14—5:10 that stands out to you. This could be something you're intrigued by, something that makes you uncomfortable, something that puzzles you, something that resonates with you, or just something you want to examine further. Write that here. What strikes you about this verse?

Going Deeper

From the Commentary

> Aaron was a "high priest," but Jesus Christ is the *Great High Priest*. No Old Testament priest could assume that title. But in what does our Lord's greatness consist?
>
> To begin with, Jesus Christ is both God and man. He is "Jesus, the Son of God." The name *Jesus* means "Savior" and identifies His humanity and His ministry on earth. "Son of God" affirms His deity and the fact that He is God. In His unique person, Jesus Christ unites deity and humanity, so that He can bring people to God and bring to people all that God has for them.
>
> —*Be Confident,* page 60

3. Why would the readers of Hebrews have any doubts about Jesus' superior title? What sort of persecution or other challenges might they have been facing that caused them to wonder?

From the Commentary

> These Hebrew Christians were tempted to give up their
> confession of faith in Christ and their confidence in Him
> (see Heb. 3:6, 14). It was not a matter of giving up their
> salvation, since salvation through Christ is eternal (Heb.
> 5:9). It was a matter of their public confession of faith.
>
> —*Be Confident,* page 61

4. What are examples of a "public confession of faith" today? Why are
Christians sometimes hesitant to publicly confess their faith?

From the History Books

Throughout history, there have been a number of religious movements that
gave special importance to Jesus but did not see Him as both completely
God and completely human. The Ebionites, an early Jewish-Christian community, believed that Jesus was not divine but became God's Son at His
baptism. Some of the Gnostics believed that Jesus was a human who became
possessed by the Spirit of Christ during His baptism. And the Marcionites
believed that Jesus was fully divine and not human at all.

5. What do you think led to these different interpretations of Jesus' role in God's plan for salvation? What happens to our understanding of salvation if Jesus is not fully divine? What happens if He is not fully human?

From the Commentary

> The very existence of a priesthood and a system of sacrifices gave evidence that man is estranged from God. It was an act of grace on God's part that He instituted the whole Levitical system. Today, that system is fulfilled in the ministry of Jesus Christ. He is both the sacrifice and the High Priest who ministers to God's people on the basis of His once-for-all offering on the cross.
>
> —*Be Confident,* page 63

6. What does the author of Hebrews tell us in 5:1–4 about God's role in the Levitical system (the Jewish system of temple sacrifices)? What does he tells us in 4:16—5:10 about God's role in Jesus' ministry? Why might this have been difficult for the early Christians to understand?

From the Commentary

> The reason Jesus Christ can be "a priest forever" is that He belongs to the "order of Melchizedek." As far as the Old Testament record is concerned, Melchizedek did not die (see Heb. 7:1–3). Of course, because he was a real man, he did die at some time, but the record is not given to us.
>
> —*Be Confident,* page 64

7. To us, Melchizedek may seem an obscure reference, but not to the first readers of this letter. Long before Moses, he was a Canaanite priest-king in a city that centuries later became Jerusalem (Gen. 14:17–20). Psalm 110:4 refers to him as if he were the head of an order of Jerusalem priests older than Moses' brother, Aaron. How is Melchizedek a symbolic picture of Jesus Christ?

What does this relationship between Melchizedek and Christ (who lived about two thousand years apart) tell you about how God has orchestrated every aspect of this history?

From the Commentary

> You would think that one sinner would have compas-
> sion for another sinner, but this is not always the case.
> Sin makes a person selfish. Sin can blind us to the hurts of
> others. Sin can harden our hearts and make us judgmen-
> tal instead of sympathetic.
>
> —*Be Confident,* page 65

8. What are some examples of what Wiersbe writes above? How does the
author of Hebrews describe Jesus' compassion in contrast to this (4:15–16)?
Why does Jesus' sympathy make a difference in His priesthood?

*More to Consider: Read Jesus' Gethsemane prayer in Luke 22:42.
What was He really praying? Why does the writer of Hebrews state
that Jesus' prayer was "heard"? How is this significant to his argument
about Jesus' unique priesthood?*

From the Commentary

> No matter what trials we meet, Jesus Christ is able to understand our needs and help us. We need never doubt His ability to sympathize and strengthen. It is also worth noting that sometimes God puts us through difficulties that we might better understand the needs of others, and become able to encourage them (see 2 Cor. 1:8ff.).
>
> —*Be Confident,* page 67

9. Reread Hebrews 5:8–10. How does Jesus' suffering and sympathy help Christians to have confidence in God?

From the Commentary

> It would be foolish for anyone to return to the inferiorities of the old law when he could enjoy the superiorities of Jesus Christ. Then why were these Hebrew believers tempted to go back into legalism? *Because they were not going on to maturity in Christ!*
>
> —*Be Confident,* page 69

10. In what ways have you seen the church today miss out on growing in maturity in Christ? Why do Christians stop growing in maturity? What are some ways to jump-start that maturity?

Looking Inward

Take a moment to reflect on all that you've explored thus far in this study of Hebrews 4:14—5:10. Review your notes and answers and think about how each of these things matters in your life today.

Tips for Small Groups: To get the most out of this section, form pairs or trios and have group members take turns answering these questions. Be honest and as open as you can in this discussion, but most of all, be encouraging and supportive of others. Be sensitive to those who are going through particularly difficult times and don't press people to speak if they're uncomfortable doing so.

11. How comfortable are you with publicly confessing your faith? In what circumstances, if any, are you uncomfortable about your faith? Why?

12. Have you ever shown a lack of compassion for another sinner? If so, what prompted that feeling? How does it feel to know that, because of His humanity, Jesus truly understands your circumstances? How can this build your confidence in Him?

13. What role does fear or doubt play in your ability to grow in maturity? What, if anything, have you found so far in Hebrews that helps you overcome fear or doubt?

Going Forward

14. Think of one or two things that you have learned that you'd like to work on in the coming week. Remember that this is all about quality, not quantity. It's better to work on one specific area of life and do it well than to work on many and do poorly (or to be so overwhelmed that you simply

don't try). Remember also that Christ, your High Priest, is available to help you.

Do you need to build confidence in publicly acknowledging your faith or taking risks to serve Christ? Do you need to work on growing in maturity and trusting Jesus as High Priest? Be specific. Go back through Hebrews 4:14—5:10 and put a star next to the phrase or verse that is most encouraging to you. Consider memorizing this verse.

Real-Life Application Ideas: Spend some time exploring the role of the high priest in Jewish history. As you examine the role the high priest played in biblical times, consider how Jesus plays this role for you in everyday life. What does it look like to live a life of faith, trusting that Jesus has paid the price for your sins and is greater than any hardship you face?

Seeking Help

15. Write a prayer below (or simply pray one in silence), inviting God to work on your mind and heart in those areas you've previously noted. Be honest about your desires and fears.

Notes for Small Groups:

- *Look for ways to put into practice the things you wrote in the Going Forward section. Talk with other group members about your ideas and commit to being accountable to one another.*

- *During the coming week, ask the Holy Spirit to continue to reveal truth to you from what you've read and studied.*

- *Before you start the next lesson, read Hebrews 5:11— 6:20. For more in-depth lesson preparation, read chapter 5, "Pilgrims Should Make Progress," in* Be Confident.

Don't Be Lazy!
(HEBREWS 5:11—6:20)

Before you begin ...
- *Pray for the Holy Spirit to reveal truth and wisdom as you go through this lesson.*
- *Read Hebrews 5:11—6:20. This lesson references chapter 5 in* Be Confident. *It will be helpful for you to have your Bible and a copy of the commentary available as you work through this lesson.*

Getting Started

From the Commentary

"We do not want you to become lazy, but to imitate those who through faith and patience inherit what has been promised" (Heb. 6:12 NIV).

This verse summarizes the main message of this difficult (and often misunderstood) section of the epistle. Israel wanted to go back to Egypt, and, as a result, a whole generation failed to inherit what God had promised. They were safely delivered out of Egypt, but they never enjoyed the promised rest in Canaan.

—*Be Confident,* page 73

1. What are some ways Christians become lazy today? What causes that laziness?

More to Consider: Think about the spiritual progress your church has made since you began attending. What are the marks of spiritual progression? What are the marks of a faith-lazy church?

2. Choose one verse or phrase from Hebrews 5:11—6:20 that stands out to you. This could be something you're intrigued by, something that makes you uncomfortable, something that puzzles you, something that resonates with you, or just something you want to examine further. Write that here. What strikes you about this verse?

Going Deeper

From the Commentary

> One of the first symptoms of spiritual regression, or back-
> sliding, is a dullness toward the Bible. Sunday school class
> is dull, the preaching is dull, anything spiritual is dull. The
> problem is usually not with the Sunday school teacher or
> the pastor, but with the believer himself.
>
> —*Be Confident,* page 74

3. What are some examples of spiritual regression you've witnessed in the
church? When is the problem not with the believer, but the leadership?

From the Commentary

> The ability to share spiritual truth with others is a mark of
> maturity. Not all Christians have the gift of teaching, but
> all can share what they learn from the Word. One of the
> hardest lessons children must learn is the lesson of sharing.
> The recipients of this letter had been saved long enough to
> be able to share God's truth with others. But, instead of
> helping others to grow, these Hebrew Christians were in

need of learning *again* the simple teachings of the Christian life. They were experiencing a second childhood!

—*Be Confident,* page 74

4. Why do you think the recipients of this letter were having difficulty with
the simple teachings listed in 6:1–2? What are the internal reasons why
believers regress? What are some external pressures that might cause regression? How should we approach these challenges?

From Today's World

There is a tendency in our modern culture to "dumb down" artistic endeav-
ors in order to reach a larger audience (and therefore, potentially receive a
greater revenue). You can see this in Hollywood movies, in popular literature, and even in music. While there is certainly an audience for all kinds
of art, that which challenges participants to stretch and grow is sadly hard
to find, because most people don't want to stretch and grow.

5. The author of Hebrews is frustrated that his readers haven't moved from
the basics of faith. Where do we turn in our culture to find things that
help us grow wiser, stronger, and more mature? What does it take to grow
beyond the basics?

The author encourages his readers to grow by training themselves over time to distinguish good from evil (5:14). In practical terms, how does an individual or a Christian community train themselves to do this?

From the Commentary

> The "milk" of the Word refers to what Jesus Christ did on earth—His birth, life, teaching, death, burial, and resurrection. The "meat" of the Word refers to what Jesus Christ is now doing in heaven. We begin the Christian life on the basis of His finished work on earth. We grow in the Christian life on the basis of His unfinished work in heaven.
>
> —*Be Confident,* page 75

6. What is the "unfinished work in heaven" that the author of Hebrews wants his readers to discover? What is Jesus Christ doing now? How do believers learn about and participate in this?

From the Commentary

> If we are going to make progress, we have to leave the childhood things behind and go forward in spiritual

growth. Hebrews 6:1 literally reads, "Therefore, having left [once and for all] the elementary lessons [the ABCs] of the teaching of Christ." When I was in kindergarten, the teacher taught us our ABCs. (We didn't have television to teach us in those days.) You learn your ABCs so that you might read words, sentences, books—in fact, anything in literature. But you do not keep learning the basics.

—Be Confident, page 76

7. What are the basics of faith? How are these important to understanding the more complex issues of faith? What happens if believers throw out the basics in their attempts to understand faith?

From the Commentary

The writer's purpose was not to frighten the readers but to assure them. If he had wanted to frighten them, he would have named whatever sin (or sins) would have caused them to disgrace Jesus Christ; but he did not do so.

—Be Confident, page 80

8. Circle the content in Hebrews 5:11—6:20 that might be "frightening" to believers. How would naming specific sins have been even more frightening? In what ways does this passage reassure readers?

More to Consider: What are the "things that accompany salvation" referenced in Hebrews 6:9?

From the Commentary

We Christians today have more of God's promises than did Abraham! What is keeping us from making spiritual progress? *We do not apply ourselves by faith.* To return to the illustration of the farm, the farmer does not reap a harvest by sitting on the porch looking at the seed. He must get busy and plow, plant, weed, cultivate, and perhaps water the soil.

—*Be Confident,* page 82

9. Describe some of the promises we have that Abraham didn't. What are some ways a community of Christians can plow, plant, weed, cultivate, and water the "soil" so that members grow and live fruitful lives?

From the Commentary

> Our hope in Christ is like an anchor for the soul. The anchor was a popular symbol in the early church. At least sixty-six pictures of anchors have been found in the catacombs. The Greek stoic philosopher Epictetus wrote, "One must not tie a ship to a single anchor, nor life to a single hope." Christians have but one anchor—Jesus Christ our hope (Col. 1:5; 1 Tim. 1:1).
>
> —*Be Confident,* page 83

10. What are some of the anchors other than Jesus that people tie themselves to? How does the author of Hebrews describe the certainty of God's promise—the anchor—in Hebrews 6:13–20?

Looking Inward

Take a moment to reflect on all that you've explored thus far in this study of Hebrews 5:11—6:20. Review your notes and answers and think about how each of these things matters in your life today.

Tips for Small Groups: To get the most out of this section, form pairs or trios and have group members take turns answering these questions. Be honest and as open as you can in this discussion, but most of all, be encouraging and supportive of others. Be sensitive to those who are going through particularly difficult times and don't press people to speak if they're uncomfortable doing so.

11. When have you experienced spiritual regression, the sense that Christian faith, worship, prayer, etc., are dull? What led up to that season? How did you escape from it (if you did escape)? If you're in such a season now, what would it take to move out of it?

12. In what ways are you still studying your ABCs of faith? What are some of the more advanced parts of the Christian life you've begun to explore? What is the impetus for growing in faith?

13. What are some of the things you do to cultivate your faith? What, if anything, do you do to cultivate the faith of others?

Going Forward

14. Think of one or two things that you have learned that you'd like to work on in the coming week. Remember that this is all about quality, not quantity. It's better to work on one specific area of life and do it well than to work on many and do poorly (or to be so overwhelmed that you simply don't try). Remember also that the Holy Spirit is eager to help you grow.

Do you need to solidify your confidence in the ABCs of faith? Move beyond the basics? Be more proactive in training yourself to distinguish good from evil? Be specific. Go back through Hebrews 5:11—6:20 and put a star next to the phrase or verse that is most encouraging to you. Consider memorizing this verse.

Real-Life Application Ideas: Make an appointment to meet with your pastor or small-group leader so you can discuss how you've been progressing in your faith. Come to the meeting with an open mind, and be sure to spend more time listening than talking as you seek for ways to grow in faith.

Seeking Help

15. Write a prayer below (or simply pray one in silence), inviting God to work on your mind and heart in those areas you've previously noted. Be honest about your desires and fears.

Notes for Small Groups:

- *Look for ways to put into practice the things you wrote in the Going Forward section. Talk with other group members about your ideas and commit to being accountable to one another.*

- *During the coming week, ask the Holy Spirit to continue to reveal truth to you from what you've read and studied.*

- *Before you start the next lesson, read Hebrews 7. For more in-depth lesson preparation, read chapter 6, "Mysterious Melchizedek," in* Be Confident.

The Mystery of Melchizedek

(HEBREWS 7)

Before you begin …
- *Pray for the Holy Spirit to reveal truth and wisdom as you go through this lesson.*
- *Read Hebrews 7. This lesson references chapter 6 in* Be Confident. *It will be helpful for you to have your Bible and a copy of the commentary available as you work through this lesson.*

Getting Started

From the Commentary

If you were asked to name the most important people in the Old Testament, I doubt that Melchizedek's name would be on your list. He appeared once, in Genesis 14:17–24, and he was referred to once more, in Psalm 110:4. You could hardly call this "top billing." But the Holy Spirit reached back into the Old Testament and used those two passages to present a most important truth: The priesthood of Jesus Christ is superior to that of Aaron because "the order of Melchizedek" is superior to "the order of Levi." …

The Jewish nation was accustomed to the priesthood of the tribe of Levi. This tribe was chosen by God to serve in the tabernacle (Ex. 29; Num. 18). Aaron was the first high priest, appointed by God. In spite of their many failures, the priests had served God for centuries, but now the writer has affirmed that their priesthood has ended!

—*Be Confident,* pages 87–88

1. What do you think the initial reaction would have been to this chapter of the letter? How has the church in general responded to sudden revelations that "things are different than they once were"?

More to Consider: Read Genesis 14:17–24. How does this event relate to what the author of Hebrews is presenting in chapter 7?

2. Choose one verse or phrase from Hebrews 7 that stands out to you. This could be something you're intrigued by, something that makes you

uncomfortable, something that puzzles you, something that resonates with you, or just something you want to examine further. Write that here. What strikes you about this verse?

Going Deeper

From the Commentary

> In the Bible, names and their meanings are often important. We name our children today without much consideration for what their names mean, but this was not the case in Bible days. Sometimes a great spiritual crisis was the occasion for changing a person's name (see Gen. 32:24–32; John 1:35–42). The name *Melchizedek* means "king of righteousness" in the Hebrew language. The word *Salem* means "peace" (the Hebrew word *shalom*), so that Melchizedek is "king of peace" as well as "king of righteousness."
>
> —*Be Confident*, page 88

3. What, if anything, is surprising to you about Melchizedek's name? How is this name significant to the argument the author of Hebrews is making?

How might you describe this as the work of the Holy Spirit instead of mere coincidence?

From the Commentary

> True peace can be experienced only on the basis of righteousness. If we want to enjoy "peace with God," we must be "justified [declared righteous] by faith" (Rom. 5:1). Man cannot produce righteousness by keeping the Old Testament law (Gal. 2:21). It is only through the work of Jesus Christ on the cross that righteousness and peace could have "kissed each other."
>
> —*Be Confident*, page 89

4. Why can true peace only be experienced on the "basis of righteousness"? What is peace without justice? Some people believe God offers us peace with Him just because He loves us, and there was no need for Jesus to die to make that happen. What's appealing about that thinking? What's wrong with that thinking?

From Today's World

One of the more popular books in recent years is *The Da Vinci Code*. While it was clearly identified as a work of fiction, the content of this novel sparked all kinds of debate. Once-hidden religious "secrets" are the basis for much of the complex story line, and those caused quite a controversy among believers and nonbelievers attempting to unravel truth from fiction. *The Da Vinci Code* was not unique—many works of a similar ilk preceded and followed this novel—but there is no question that this particular book brought the topic of "hidden things" into the minds of many.

5. What is the appeal of novels that purport to reveal ancient religious secrets? How does this sort of "revelation" compare to what the author of Hebrews is teaching about Melchizedek? What is the best barometer of veracity when considering secrets or hidden things of the Christian faith?

From the Commentary

Melchizedek was not an angel or some superhuman creature; nor was he an Old Testament appearance of Jesus Christ. He was a real man, a real king, and a real priest in a real city. But *as far as the record is concerned*, he was not born, nor did he die.

—*Be Confident,* page 90

6. How is Melchizedek's story a picture of Jesus? Why do you think the Bible includes the story of Melchizedek? Why would this have been particularly significant to the Hebrews reading this letter?

From the Commentary

> Since Jesus Christ is Priest *forever*, and since He has a nature to match that eternal priesthood, He can never be replaced. The annulling (Heb. 7:18, "disannulling") of the law meant the abolishing of the priesthood. But nobody can annul "the power of an endless life"! The logic holds: Jesus Christ is a Priest forever.
>
> —*Be Confident,* page 92

7. Why is it critical to note that Jesus is a priest forever (7:24–25)? How would this have been received by the Hebrews? What are the implications of a "forever priest" for us today?

From the Commentary

> In Hebrews 7:22, we have the first occurrence of a very important word in Hebrews—*testament.* This word, which is usually translated "covenant," is used twenty-one times in the letter, and it is the equivalent of "last will and testament."
>
> —*Be Confident,* page 94

8. Underline or list all the uses of the word *testament* or *covenant* in Hebrews. (A concordance will help you here.) Why is this such a key word, particularly in chapter 7?

More to Consider: Compare Jesus' "last will and testament" with earthly wills. (Perhaps you've had experience with the illegal handling of a will, for example.) How is Jesus' testament unique?

From the Commentary

> The basis for … salvation is the heavenly intercession of
> the Savior.…
>
> Intercession involves our Lord's representation of His peo-
> ple at the throne of God. Through Christ, believers are
> able to draw near to God in prayer and also to offer spiri-
> tual sacrifices to God (Heb. 4:14–16; 1 Peter 2:5). It has
> well been said that Christ's life in heaven is His prayer for
> us. It is what He *is* that determines what He *does*.
>
> —*Be Confident,* page 95

9. When Jesus prays for you before His Father's throne, what do you think
He's saying? What sort of "spiritual sacrifices" can we offer to God because
of Christ's intercession? How do we do this through Jesus?

From the Commentary

> No matter how devoted and obedient the Aaronic priests
> were, they could not always meet the needs of all the peo-
> ple. But Jesus Christ perfectly meets all of our needs.
>
> —*Be Confident,* page 96

10. What are some of the needs the Aaronic priests could not meet (7:26–28)? What are examples today of needs that man can't meet, but Jesus can? How do we practically go about counting on Jesus to meet those needs?

Looking Inward

Take a moment to reflect on all that you've explored thus far in this study of Hebrews 7. Review your notes and answers and think about how each of these things matters in your life today.

Tips for Small Groups: To get the most out of this section, form pairs or trios and have group members take turns answering these questions. Be honest and as open as you can in this discussion, but most of all, be encouraging and supportive of others. Be sensitive to those who are going through particularly difficult times and don't press people to speak if they're uncomfortable doing so.

11. How well do you respond to change? What might your response have been to the sudden revelation that the priesthood of Aaron was no longer valid? What are some similar revelations you've experienced in your life of faith?

12. In what ways have you experienced true peace with God or because of God? How have you tried to find peace on your own? What does "righteousness" mean to you? What role does the concept play in your life?

13. When you think of Jesus as your priest now and forever, what about that image is difficult to comprehend? What about it is helpful to you?

Going Forward

14. Think of one or two things that you have learned that you'd like to work on in the coming week. Remember that this is all about quality, not quantity. It's better to work on one specific area of life and do it well than to work on many and do poorly (or to be so overwhelmed that you simply don't try).

Do you need to work on being comfortable with change? On learning what it means to trust Jesus as your priest? Be specific. Go back through Hebrews 7 and put a star next to the phrase or verse that is most encouraging to you. Consider memorizing this verse.

Real-Life Application Ideas: The role of priest might be unfamiliar to you or tinged by connotations that aren't particularly positive. Spend a little time researching the history of the Aaronic priesthood, then take a close look at Jesus' role as eternal priest. How does Jesus' role affect the everyday?

Seeking Help

15. Write a prayer below (or simply pray one in silence), inviting God to work on your mind and heart in those areas you've previously noted. Be honest about your desires and fears.

Notes for Small Groups:

• *Look for ways to put into practice the things you wrote in the Going Forward section. Talk with other group members about your ideas and commit to being accountable to one another.*

• *During the coming week, ask the Holy Spirit to continue to reveal truth to you from what you've read and studied.*

• *Before you start the next lesson, read Hebrews 8. For more in-depth lesson preparation, read chapter 7, "The Better Covenant," in* Be Confident.

The Best Covenant
(HEBREWS 8)

Before you begin ...
- *Pray for the Holy Spirit to reveal truth and wisdom as you go through this lesson.*
- *Read Hebrews 8. This lesson references chapter 7 in* Be Confident. *It will be helpful for you to have your Bible and a copy of the commentary available as you work through this lesson.*

Getting Started

From the Commentary

I once spoke at a meeting of religious broadcasters at which a friend of mine was to provide the ministry of music. He is a superb pianist with a gift for interpreting Christian music, and I have always enjoyed listening to him. But that day my heart went out to him in sympathy, because the motel had provided the most deteriorated and derelict piano I have ever seen. It must have been donated by a local wrecking company. My friend did his best, but it would have been much better had he been playing a decent instrument.

Jesus Christ is God's superior Priest, but is there anything that can minimize this superiority? Nothing! For He ministers on the basis of a better covenant (Heb. 8).

—*Be Confident,* page 101

1. What are some examples of things you've experienced that are "less than the best"? How might the Hebrews have experienced this with regard even to the priests? In what ways would this news that there is a "better covenant" have been good news for the Hebrews?

More to Consider: There were no chairs in the Old Testament tabernacle because the work of the priests was never finished. But Jesus' sacrifice completed the work. How would the Jewish Christians have received this once-and-for-all sacrifice? What joy would they have discovered in it? What would have been difficult to accept or understand?

2. Choose one verse or phrase from Hebrews 8 that stands out to you. This could be something you're intrigued by, something that makes you uncomfortable, something that puzzles you, something that resonates with you, or just something you want to examine further. Write that here. What strikes you about this verse?

Going Deeper

From the Commentary

> Jesus Christ, in His ascension and exaltation, "passed through the heavens" (Heb. 4:14 NASB). He is now exalted as high as anyone could be (Eph. 1:20–23; Phil. 2:5–11).
>
> —*Be Confident,* page 103

3. Read the above passages from Ephesians and Philippians. Why is it important that Jesus has ascended to the highest place, at the Father's right hand (Heb. 8:1–2)? How does this make His covenant better than the one lived out in the earthly temple in Jerusalem?

From the Commentary

> We must not, however, get the impression that our Lord
> is offering sacrifices in heaven that correspond to the Old
> Testament sacrifices. The word *somewhat* in Hebrews 8:3
> is in the singular, and the phrase *to offer* is in a Greek tense
> that implies "offer once and for all."
>
> —*Be Confident,* page 104

4. Why does it matter that Jesus offered Himself as the sacrifice once and
for all? Like the animals that were sacrificed under the Aaronic system, Jesus
died. But unlike them, He was resurrected. How does that make His covenant and His promises better (8:6)?

From Today's World

The word *covenant* has seen little use outside of the church context in recent
years except where it comes to legal issues and homeowners' associations. In
the latter usage, it refers to an agreed-upon set of rules or guidelines restrict-
ing certain homeowner activities (such as limiting the exterior colors for
homes, the number of vehicles allowed outside a garage, general cleanli-
ness, etc.).

5. In what ways do people play "fast and loose" with homeowners' covenants? How does our understanding of the word *covenant* affect our understanding of Hebrews 8? What are the key differences between our modern understanding of the word *covenant* and the usage in Scripture?

From the Commentary

> Moses was the mediator (go-between) of the old covenant in the giving of the law (Gal. 3:19–20). The people of Israel were so frightened at Mount Sinai that they begged Moses to speak to them so that they would not have to hear God speak (Ex. 20:18–21). Sad to say, this fear of God did not last long, for the people soon disobeyed the very law they promised to keep.
>
> —*Be Confident,* page 106

6. Why do you think the people were so quick to disobey the law Moses brought to them from God? If they were so afraid of God, what changed?

From the Commentary

> The church today is made up of regenerated Jews and
> Gentiles who are one body in Christ (Eph. 2:11–22;
> Gal. 3:27–29). All who are "in Christ" share in the new
> covenant, which was purchased on the cross. Today the
> blessings of the new covenant are applied to individu-
> als. When Jesus comes in glory to redeem Israel, then the
> blessings of the new covenant will be applied to that belea-
> guered nation.
>
> —*Be Confident,* page 108

7. Hebrews 8:8–12 quotes Jeremiah 31:31–34. According to these verses,
how is the new covenant superior to the old one? Read the rest of Jeremiah
31. What plans does God have for Israel? How do these plans line up with
the new covenant as established by Jesus?

From the Commentary

> God did not find fault with His covenant but with His
> people. "Wherefore the law is holy, and the command-
> ment holy, and just, and good" (Rom. 7:12). The problem

is not with the law, but with our sinful natures, for by ourselves we cannot keep God's law.

—*Be Confident,* page 109

8. What makes the law "holy"? Why did God give the law in the first place if He knew we could not keep it by ourselves? What does this tell you about the way in which God works?

From the Commentary

Even though the new covenant of grace brings with it freedom from the law of Moses (Gal. 5:1), it does not bring freedom to disobey God and to sin. God still desires that the "righteousness of the law" should be fulfilled in us through the ministry of the Holy Spirit (Rom. 8:1–4). There is a lawful use of the law (1 Tim. 1:8–11)....

The law was external; God's demands were written on tablets of stone. But the new covenant makes it possible for God's Word to be written on human minds and hearts (2 Cor. 3:1–3). God's grace makes possible an internal transformation that makes a surrendered believer more and more like Jesus Christ (2 Cor. 3:18).

—*Be Confident,* pages 108, 110

9. Hebrews 8:10 speaks of God's law not thrown away but written on our hearts. How does God write His law on our hearts? Are we passive as God writes the law on our hearts? Or do we make some active response? Please explain how this works.

10. Is there a role for external laws/rules/commands in all of this? If so, what is it? If not, why not?

More to Consider: Read Hebrews 8:7–9. What does this passage tell us about God's grace?

Looking Inward

Take a moment to reflect on all that you've explored thus far in this study of Hebrews 8. Review your notes and answers and think about how each of these things matters in your life today.

Tips for Small Groups: To get the most out of this section, form pairs or trios and have group members take turns answering these questions. Be honest and as open as you can in this discussion, but most of all, be encouraging and supportive of others. Be sensitive to those who are going through particularly difficult times and don't press people to speak if they're uncomfortable doing so.

11. What about the new covenant is difficult for you to comprehend? What about it makes you feel confident to act in faith?

12. Is God writing His law on your heart? If so, describe that process. Is there anything you need to do to cooperate in that process? If so, what?

13. In what ways have you been like the Israelites who quickly disobeyed God's law? How is your circumstance under the new covenant different from theirs? What difference does it make to you today that Jesus is the final sacrifice for your sins?

Going Forward

14. Think of one or two things that you have learned that you'd like to work on in the coming week. Remember that this is all about quality, not quantity. It's better to work on one specific area of life and do it well than to work on many and do poorly (or to be so overwhelmed that you simply don't try).

Do you need to better cooperate with God as He writes His law on your heart? Do you need to cultivate confidence that Jesus really is the final sacrifice for your sin? Do you need to picture Him next to the Father, above all else in the universe, interceding for you? Be specific. Go back through Hebrews 8 and put a star next to the phrase or verse that is most encouraging to you. Consider memorizing this verse.

Real-Life Application Ideas: Consider all the "covenants" you and those you love experience in the everyday—commitments to do things or avoid certain behaviors in family, work, or social situations. How well are you following through on these? In what ways are these sorts of promises like the old covenant? Consider what it would take to make them look more like the new covenant—the covenant of grace.

Seeking Help

15. Write a prayer below (or simply pray one in silence), inviting God to work on your mind and heart in those areas you've previously noted. Be honest about your desires and fears.

Notes for Small Groups:

- *Look for ways to put into practice the things you wrote in the Going Forward section. Talk with other group members about your ideas and commit to being accountable to one another.*

- *During the coming week, ask the Holy Spirit to continue to reveal truth to you from what you've read and studied.*

- *Before you start the next lesson, read Hebrews 9. For more in-depth lesson preparation, read chapter 8, "The Superior Sanctuary," in* Be Confident.

The Heavenly Sanctuary

(HEBREWS 9)

Before you begin ...
- *Pray for the Holy Spirit to reveal truth and wisdom as you go through this lesson.*
- *Read Hebrews 9. This lesson references chapter 8 in* Be Confident. *It will be helpful for you to have your Bible and a copy of the commentary available as you work through this lesson.*

Getting Started

From the Commentary

The Christian is a citizen of two worlds, the earthly and the heavenly. He must render to Caesar the things that are Caesar's and to God the things that are God's (Matt. 22:21). Because he is a citizen of two worlds, he must learn how to walk by faith in a world that is governed by sight....

This principle of faith must apply to our relationship to the heavenly sanctuary.

—*Be Confident,* page 115

1. What does it look like in practical terms to "walk in two worlds"? Give an example.

More to Consider: Read the following Scripture passages: Acts 7:45–50; John 4:19–24; Isaiah 57:15; Isaiah 66:1–2. What do these passages tell us about God's dwelling place in the old covenant and in the new covenant?

2. Choose one verse or phrase from Hebrews 9 that stands out to you. This could be something you're intrigued by, something that makes you uncomfortable, something that puzzles you, something that resonates with you, or just something you want to examine further. Write that here. What strikes you about this verse?

Going Deeper

From the Commentary

> While the old covenant was in force, the ministry of the
> priests was ordained of God and perfectly proper.
>
> —*Be Confident,* page 116

3. If everything about the old, earthly sanctuary was according to God's
will, what made it inferior to the new, heavenly sanctuary (9:1–14)?

From the Commentary

> The writer listed the various parts and furnishings of the
> tabernacle because each of these carried a spiritual meaning.
> They were "patterns of things in the heavens" (Heb. 9:23).
>
> —*Be Confident,* page 116

4. Why does the writer of Hebrews go into such detail in 9:1–5 and then
suddenly state "we cannot discuss these things in detail now"? Why discuss
them in the first place? In what ways do these descriptions set the stage for
his explanation of the new sanctuary?

From Today's World

If you've ever worked in a cubicle or for a large company where privacy is not easy to come by, you've probably witnessed (or been privy to) a closed-door meeting. Such meetings could signal anything from impending company changes, to specific employee chastisement, to firings, to birthday-party planning. The only consistent factor in such meetings is that some people are excluded from access to the conversation. This idea of limited access to conversation is not unlike the way the Israelites lived during the Aaronic priesthood. Only the high priest himself could enter the Holy of Holies to speak with God and only once a year.

5. How might this limited access have made the rest of the Israelites feel about their relationship with God? Was there anything valuable they could have learned about God from this limited access? If so, what? Why might the change from limited to full access have been difficult for the Jewish priests to accept?

From the Commentary

The sacrifices offered and the blood applied to the mercy seat could never change the heart or the conscience of a worshipper. All of the ceremonies associated with the tabernacle had to do with ceremonial purity, not moral purity. They were "carnal ordinances" that pertained to the outer man but that could not change the inner man.

—*Be Confident,* page 120

6. What's the difference between "ceremonial" and "moral" purity? Why is this difference important to note?

From the Commentary

We need no proof that the blood of Jesus Christ is far superior to that of animal sacrifices. How can the blood of *animals* ever solve the problem of *humans'* sins?

—*Be Confident,* page 121

7. Why do you think God chose to have the priests sacrifice animals to solve the problem of humans' sins? Do you think God already had Jesus' sacrifice in mind when He gave Moses the instructions for the animal sacrifices? Why or why not?

From the Commentary

> This verse (Heb. 9:15) makes it clear that there was no
> final and complete redemption under the old covenant.
> Those transgressions were *covered* by the blood of the
> many sacrifices, but not *cleansed* until the sacrifice of Jesus
> Christ on the cross (Rom. 3:24–26).
>
> —*Be Confident,* page 122

8. What is the difference between being "covered" by the blood of animal
sacrifices and being "cleansed"? How does a person live if she is confident
that Jesus has cleansed her conscience (9:14)? What are some ways Christians today continue to try to offer sacrifices to cover their sins?

From the Commentary

> Through Jesus Christ, we who are sinners can enter into the
> Holy of Holies in the heavenly sanctuary (Heb. 10:19–22).
> Physically, of course, we are on earth, but spiritually, we
> are communing with God in the heavenly Holy of Holies.
> In order for God to receive us into this heavenly fellow-
> ship, the blood of Jesus Christ *had to be applied.*
>
> —*Be Confident,* page 124

9. How do we enter the heavenly sanctuary? What challenges do believers face as we attempt to live our earthly lives while communing with God in the Holy of Holies? What role does the Holy Spirit play in our ability to do this?

From the Commentary

> Beware of trusting anything for your spiritual life that is "made with hands" (Heb. 9:24). It will not last. The tabernacle was replaced by Solomon's temple, and that temple was destroyed by the Babylonians. When the Jews returned to their land after the captivity, they rebuilt their temple, and King Herod, in later years, expanded and embellished it. But the Romans destroyed that temple, and it has never been rebuilt.
>
> —*Be Confident*, page 124

10. What sorts of things do Christians sometimes trust that are "made with hands"? How should we relate to man-made things like church buildings or church programs?

Looking Inward

Take a moment to reflect on all that you've explored thus far in this study of Hebrews 9. Review your notes and answers and think about how each of these things matters in your life today.

Tips for Small Groups: To get the most out of this section, form pairs or trios and have group members take turns answering these questions. Be honest and as open as you can in this discussion, but most of all, be encouraging and supportive of others. Be sensitive to those who are going through particularly difficult times and don't press people to speak if they're uncomfortable doing so.

11. When you consider the old sanctuary and the limited access to God's presence, what is the first thought that comes to mind? Is communing with God in the heavenly sanctuary a reality for you or just a theory? Reflect on your experience.

12. What does it mean to you that you have been both covered and cleansed by the blood of Christ? How do you deal with ongoing sins in light of Jesus' once-and-for-all sacrifice?

13. Think about the church you attend now. Are there any ways you put too much stock in the building or other human-made things? If so, what would it take to change that perspective?

Going Forward

14. Think of one or two things that you have learned that you'd like to work on in the coming week. Remember that this is all about quality, not quantity. It's better to work on one specific area of life and do it well than to work on many and do poorly (or to be so overwhelmed that you simply don't try).

Do you need to work on approaching God confidently, knowing that there is no longer a curtain separating you from His presence? Do you need to reflect on what it means practically to commune with God in the heavenly Holy of Holies? Be specific. Go back through Hebrews 9 and put a star next to the phrase or verse that is most encouraging to you. Consider memorizing this verse.

Real-Life Application Ideas: Take inventory of those material things you put your faith in. Then review each one to see if your faith is perhaps misplaced. What are ways you can move from trusting "things" to trusting Jesus and those things that are not temporary?

Seeking Help

15. Write a prayer below (or simply pray one in silence), inviting God to work on your mind and heart in those areas you've previously noted. Be honest about your desires and fears.

Notes for Small Groups:

- *Look for ways to put into practice the things you wrote in the Going Forward section. Talk with other group members about your ideas and commit to being accountable to one another.*

- *During the coming week, ask the Holy Spirit to continue to reveal truth to you from what you've read and studied.*

- *Before you start the next lesson, read Hebrews 10. For more in-depth lesson preparation, read chapter 9, "The Superior Sacrifice," in* Be Confident.

Perfect Sacrifice
(HEBREWS 10)

Before you begin ...
- *Pray for the Holy Spirit to reveal truth and wisdom as you go through this lesson.*
- *Read Hebrews 10. This lesson references chapter 9 in* Be Confident. *It will be helpful for you to have your Bible and a copy of the commentary available as you work through this lesson.*

Getting Started

From the Commentary

The tenth chapter of Hebrews emphasizes the perfect sacrifice of Jesus Christ, in contrast with the imperfect sacrifices that were offered under the old covenant. Our Lord's superior priesthood belongs to a better order—Melchizedek's and not Aaron's. It functions on the basis of a better covenant—the new covenant—and in a better sanctuary, in heaven. But all of this depends on the better sacrifice, which is the theme of this chapter.

—*Be Confident,* page 130

1. Why do the better order, covenant, and sanctuary depend on the better sacrifice? As you read through Hebrews 10, what emotions did you experience? How do you think the first readers of this letter would have felt upon reading this chapter?

More to Consider: Respond to the following statement: "We are not sinners because we sin. We sin because we are sinners." How does this fit with the message of Hebrews 10?

2. Choose one verse or phrase from Hebrews 10 that stands out to you. This could be something you're intrigued by, something that makes you uncomfortable, something that puzzles you, something that resonates with you, or just something you want to examine further. Write that here. What strikes you about this verse?

Going Deeper

From the Commentary

> The very *nature* of the old covenant sacrifices made them inferior. The law was only "a shadow of good things to come" and not the reality itself. The sacrificial system was a type or picture of the work our Lord would accomplish on the cross. This meant that the system was temporary, and therefore could accomplish nothing permanent. The very repetition of the sacrifices day after day, and the Day of Atonement year after year, pointed out the entire system's weaknesses.
>
> —*Be Confident,* page 130

3. Do you think the Jews of Jesus' day knew that the system of sacrifices was temporary? What makes you say that? Why didn't Jesus' fellow Jews all immediately see His sacrifice as the final answer to the problem of sin?

From the Commentary

> Jesus came to do the Father's will. This will is the new covenant that has replaced the old covenant. Through His

death and resurrection, Jesus Christ has taken away the first covenant and established the second. The readers of this epistle called Hebrews would get the message: Why go back to a covenant that has been taken away? Why go back to sacrifices that are inferior?

—*Be Confident,* pages 132–33

4. Like the first readers of this letter, we live in a world of rapid change. How can we discern when old ways are superior and when they are inferior? What are some good criteria for evaluating new versus old?

Give an example of an aspect of tradition that you think is important to continue practicing. Why do you think it's worth keeping? Then give an example of a way you think Christians need to adapt to a changing culture. Why do you think that's an area where new is better?

From the History Books

Animal sacrifice was not unique to Jewish culture—it was practiced by the Aztecs, Romans, and Greeks, among others. The ancient Egyptians, however, did not practice animal sacrifice. Some cultures (the Canaanites, Aztecs, and Druids, for example) sacrificed humans. In most cases, the motivation for animal or human sacrifice was to appease the gods or affect nature in ways seen as crucial for the community's survival. The moral dimension of Jewish sacrifice—that it was aimed at dealing with human failure to obey moral laws—made it unique in the ancient world. None of these cultures conceived of a once-and-for-all sacrifice of either animals or a human being.

5. How is the moral dimension crucial for understanding Jesus' sacrifice?

6. The Jews saw human sacrifice as a pagan abomination. How might this attitude have affected their response to the idea of Jesus as the sacrifice for their sins?

In our culture animal sacrifice is abhorrent, and human sacrifice even worse. How do you think that affects a modern person who reads Hebrews to understand what Jesus did?

From the Commentary

> On the basis of these assurances [in Hebrews]—that we have boldness to enter because we have a living High Priest—we have an "open invitation" to enter the presence of God.
>
> —*Be Confident,* page 135

7. Circle or list the assurances in Hebrews 10. What would have been exciting to the early believers about having access to the presence of God? What might have been daunting? How is that similar today?

From the Commentary

> When a believer has his hope fixed on Christ and relies on the faithfulness of God, then he will not waver. Instead of looking back (as the Jews so often did), we should look ahead to the coming of the Lord.
>
> *—Be Confident,* page 136

8. Read Hebrews 10:23. What does it mean to "hold unswervingly" to the hope? How do we look ahead to the coming of the Lord while also living in the now?

More to Consider: Circle the three Christian virtues of faith, hope, and love in Hebrews 10:22–24. How are they used in this context?

From the Commentary

> How does an arrogant attitude affect a believer's relationship with God? It is as though he treads Jesus Christ underfoot, cheapens the precious blood that saved him ("an unholy thing" [Heb. 10:29] = "a common thing"), and insults the Holy Spirit.
>
> *—Be Confident,* page 137

9. Summarize in your own words the exhortation in Hebrews 10:19–25. Summarize the exhortation in Hebrews 10:26–31. How are the two connected?

What are some of the arrogant attitudes believers may have toward God? Where do they come from? How should we respond to them?

From the Commentary

What should a believer do who has drifted away into spiritual doubt and dullness and is deliberately despising God's Word? He should turn to God for mercy and forgiveness. There is no other sacrifice for sin, but the sacrifice Christ made is sufficient for all our sins.

—*Be Confident,* page 138

10. Why is it difficult to turn to God for mercy and forgiveness after a season of drifting? What fears keep us from running back to God? How do we overcome those fears?

Looking Inward

Take a moment to reflect on all that you've explored thus far in this study of Hebrews 10. Review your notes and answers and think about how each of these things matters in your life today.

Tips for Small Groups: To get the most out of this section, form pairs or trios and have group members take turns answering these questions. Be honest and as open as you can in this discussion, but most of all, be encouraging and supportive of others. Be sensitive to those who are going through particularly difficult times and don't press people to speak if they're uncomfortable doing so.

11. How does Jesus' complete sacrifice on the cross affect the way you live your life daily? How might your life be different if the old covenant and the old way of sacrifice were still in effect today?

12. As you read through the exhortations in Hebrews 10, what stood out to you as the most personally convicting? Why do you think that hit so close to home? What action, if any, does it prompt you to take?

13. Have you ever become arrogant toward God? If so, when? What led to that arrogant attitude? How did you return to God? Was that easy or difficult? Explain.

Going Forward

14. Think of one or two things that you have learned that you'd like to work on in the coming week. Remember that this is all about quality, not quantity. It's better to work on one specific area of life and do it well than to work on many and do poorly (or to be so overwhelmed that you simply don't try).

Do you need to give some energy to accepting Jesus' sacrifice as once and for all and to living in the awareness of forgiveness? Do you need to examine your attitude so you avoid arrogance toward God? Be specific. Go back through Hebrews 10 and put a star next to the phrase or verse that is most encouraging to you. Consider memorizing this verse.

Real-Life Application Ideas: Since this chapter is all about sacrifice, take time to examine areas of your life where you might be able to respond to Jesus' sacrifice by doing something for the benefit of others—not to earn God's approval, but as an act of gratitude for what He's done for you. Look at the way you spend your time and money. Are there things you can do to positively affect others for Christ that you aren't currently doing?

Seeking Help

15. Write a prayer below (or simply pray one in silence), inviting God to work on your mind and heart in those areas you've previously noted. Be honest about your desires and fears.

Notes for Small Groups:

- *Look for ways to put into practice the things you wrote in the Going Forward section. Talk with other group members about your ideas and commit to being accountable to one another.*

- *During the coming week, ask the Holy Spirit to continue to reveal truth to you from what you've read and studied.*

- *Before you start the next lesson, read Hebrews 11. For more in-depth lesson preparation, read chapter 10, "Faith—the Greatest Power in the World," in* Be Confident.

Faith

(HEBREWS 11)

Before you begin …

- *Pray for the Holy Spirit to reveal truth and wisdom as you go through this lesson.*
- *Read Hebrews 11. This lesson references chapter 10 in* Be Confident. *It will be helpful for you to have your Bible and a copy of the commentary available as you work through this lesson.*

Getting Started

From the Commentary

The fact that Christ is a superior person (Heb. 1—6) and that He exercises a superior priesthood (Heb. 7—10) ought to encourage us to put our trust in Him. The readers of this epistle were being tempted to go back into Judaism and put their faith in Moses. Their confidence was in the visible things of this world, not the invisible realities of God. Instead of going on to perfection (maturity), they were going "back unto perdition [waste]" (Heb. 6:1; 10:39).

In Hebrews 11, all Christians are called to live by faith.

—*Be Confident,* page 143

1. How has the argument in Hebrews to this point helped to prepare for this chapter on faith? What does it mean to live by faith? How is that different from the way the Jewish people lived prior to the new covenant?

More to Consider: Before going any further, write your definition of faith. How are "faith" and "belief" different?

2. Choose one verse or phrase from Hebrews 11 that stands out to you. This could be something you're intrigued by, something that makes you uncomfortable, something that puzzles you, something that resonates with you, or just something you want to examine further. Write that here. What strikes you about this verse?

Going Deeper

From the Commentary

> Three words in Hebrews 11:1–3 summarize what true
> Bible faith is: *substance, evidence,* and *witness.* The word
> translated "substance" means literally "to stand under,
> to support." Faith is to a Christian what a foundation
> is to a house....
>
> The word *evidence* simply means "conviction." This is the
> inward conviction from God that what He has promised,
> He will perform....
>
> *Witness* ("obtained a good report") is an important word
> in Hebrews 11. It occurs not only in verse 2, but also once
> in verse 4 and once in verse 39. The summary in Hebrews
> 12:1 calls this list of men and women "so great a cloud of
> witnesses."
>
> —*Be Confident,* page 144

3. How do each of these words work together to supply a definition of faith?
Why do you think *witness* is such a key word in this passage?

From the Commentary

> Faith enables us to see what others cannot see (note Heb.
> 11:7, 13, 27). As a result, faith enables us to do what others
> cannot do! People laughed at these great men and women
> when they stepped out by faith, but God was with them
> and enabled them to succeed to His glory.
>
> —*Be Confident,* page 145

4. What are some of the things faith enabled the "cloud of witnesses" to see?
To do? What are some of the things faith enables Christians to do today?

From the History Books

In the early twentieth century, faith healing became something of national
interest with the popular rise of controversial faith healer Aimee Semple
McPherson. Others followed, but it wasn't until later in the twentieth
century and the advent of televangelism that faith healing once again was
publicly discussed among believers and nonbelievers alike.

5. How does the concept of faith healing fit in line with the teaching of
Hebrews about faith? The writer of Hebrews doesn't talk explicitly about
faith for healing. How is his discussion of faith different?

From the Commentary

> We have to admire the faith of the patriarchs. They did not have a complete Bible, and yet their faith was strong. They handed God's promises down from one generation to another. In spite of their failures and testings, these men and women believed God, and He bore witness to their faith.
>
> —*Be Confident,* page 148

6. What do the stories of the faithful in Hebrews 11 say about how God "shows up" for those who have faith? What were some of the failures they experienced? How do we hand down these stories to the next generation? Are there new stories of faith we can hand down? What are they?

From the Commentary

> God always rewards true faith—if not immediately, at least ultimately. Over against "the treasures in Egypt" Moses saw the "recompense of the reward." As Dr. Vance Havner said, "Moses chose the imperishable, saw the invisible, and did the impossible." Moses' faith enabled him to face Pharaoh unafraid, and to trust God to deal with the enemy.

The endurance of Moses was not a natural gift, for by nature Moses was hesitant and retiring. This endurance and courage came as the reward of his faith.

—*Be Confident,* page 149

7. For all that Moses did for the Israelites, he still didn't get to enter the Promised Land. What does this teach us about God's rewards for the faithful? Review the list of people in Hebrews 11. What are some other examples of rewarded faith that seem unexpected or maybe even unsatisfying (at least according to the world's understanding of "reward")?

From the Commentary

[Rahab] protected the spies, put the cord in the window as directed (Josh. 2:15–21), apparently won her family to the true faith (Josh. 2:13; 6:25), and in every way obeyed the Lord. Not only was Rahab delivered from judgment, but she became a part of the nation of Israel. She married Salmon and gave birth to Boaz who was an ancestor of King David (Matt. 1:4–6).

—*Be Confident,* page 150

8. Keeping in mind that Rahab was a pagan prostitute at the time when God chose to use her, what does her inclusion in this list of the "cloud of witnesses" tell us about God's people? About how God Himself works things for good? What do Rahab's actions teach us about the relationship between obedience and faith?

More to Consider: Check out a resource that describes the lives of great Christian martyrs. As you consider the people God has used for great things, what are the common character traits? What does the diversity of these people teach about God's plan? About how He might yet use you or those you love to further the kingdom?

From the Commentary

We would not call Samson a godly man, for he yielded to his fleshly appetites. He was a Nazarite, which meant he was dedicated to God and was never to cut his hair or partake of the fruit of the vine. (A Nazarite should not be confused with a Nazarene, a resident of Nazareth.) Samson did trust God to help and deliver him and, in the end, Samson was willing to give his life to defeat the enemy.

However, we must not conclude that believers today can expect to lead double lives and still enjoy God's blessing.

—*Be Confident,* page 151

9. Samson was impulsive, violent, and sexually promiscuous. Why do you think God chose to work through him despite these faults? How do you respond to the statement that "believers today [can't] expect to lead double lives and still enjoy God's blessing"?

From the Commentary

Faith enables us to turn from the approval of the world and seek only the approval of God. If God is glorified by delivering His people, He will do it. If He sees fit to be glorified by *not* delivering His people, then He will do that.

—*Be Confident,* page 153

10. How does faith enable us to seek only God's approval? How could God be more glorified by *not* delivering us from suffering than from delivering us from it? Does this give you confidence in God? Please explain.

Looking Inward

Take a moment to reflect on all that you've explored thus far in this study of Hebrews. Review your notes and answers and think about how each of these things matters in your life today.

Tips for Small Groups: To get the most out of this section, form pairs or trios and have group members take turns answering these questions. Be honest and as open as you can in this discussion, but most of all, be encouraging and supportive of others. Be sensitive to those who are going through particularly difficult times and don't press people to speak if they're uncomfortable doing so.

11. In what ways does the list of the faithful in Hebrews 11 encourage you? Challenge you? Intimidate you? If you were to add your own name to this list based on the way in which you've shown great faith, how would that entry read? In what areas is your faith in God currently challenged?

12. Have you ever felt that you didn't have enough faith? If so, what led to that feeling? What are some practical ways you have sought to grow in faith?

13. If you knew that you wouldn't receive any earthly rewards for your faith, how would that affect the way you live? Knowing that you will ultimately receive a promised blessing, does that make faith easier or more difficult when challenges arise?

Going Forward

14. Think of one or two things that you have learned that you'd like to work on in the coming week. Remember that this is all about quality, not quantity. It's better to work on one specific area of life and do it well than to work on many and do poorly (or to be so overwhelmed that you simply don't try).

Do you need to study more about the great patriarchs of faith? Take action to respond to God's call with faith. Be specific. Go back through Hebrews 11 and put a star next to the phrase or verse that is most encouraging to you. Consider memorizing this verse.

Real-Life Application Ideas: Ask a friend to help you evaluate areas in your life today where you could have more faith. Perhaps this is in regard to talking about Christ in conversation with a nonbelieving friend or in the way you give to the church. Talk together about how you might step out in faith in these areas, then make a plan to do this, inviting your friend to act as an accountability partner for your actions.

Seeking Help

15. Write a prayer below (or simply pray one in silence), inviting God to work on your mind and heart in those areas you've previously noted. Be honest about your desires and fears.

Notes for Small Groups:

- *Look for ways to put into practice the things you wrote in the Going Forward section. Talk with other group members about your ideas and commit to being accountable to one another.*

- *During the coming week, ask the Holy Spirit to continue to reveal truth to you from what you've read and studied.*

- *Before you start the next lesson, read Hebrews 12—13. For more in-depth lesson preparation, read chapters 11 and 12, "Stay in the Running!" and "Pardon Me, Your Faith Is Showing," in* Be Confident.

The Daily Walk
(HEBREWS 12—13)

Before you begin ...
- *Pray for the Holy Spirit to reveal truth and wisdom as you go through this lesson.*
- *Read Hebrews 12—13. This lesson references chapters 11 and 12 in* Be Confident. *It will be helpful for you to have your Bible and a copy of the commentary available as you work through this lesson.*

Getting Started

From the Commentary

The one theme that runs through this chapter is *endurance*.... The Jewish believers who received this letter were getting weary and wanted to give up; but the writer encouraged them to keep moving forward in their Christian lives, like runners on a track (see Phil. 3:12–14).

—*Be Confident,* pages 157–58

1. Circle or list all the places in Hebrews 12 that offer encouragement to endure. Why do you think the author chooses to focus on endurance after having just explored the role of faith?

More to Consider: Read Philippians 3:12–14. How does this passage compare to the message in Hebrews 12?

2. Choose one verse or phrase from Hebrews 12—13 that stands out to you. This could be something you're intrigued by, something that makes you uncomfortable, something that puzzles you, something that resonates with you, or just something you want to examine further. Write that here. What strikes you about this verse?

Going Deeper

From the Commentary

> Athletes used to wear training weights to help them pre-
> pare for the events. No athlete would actually participate
> wearing the weights because they would slow him down.
> (The modern analogy is a baseball player who swings a bat
> with a heavy metal collar on it before he steps to the plate.)
> Too much weight would tax one's endurance.
>
> —*Be Confident*, page 159

3. What are the weights Christians should remove so they can win the race?
What are some of the things that hinder a believer's progress?

From the Commentary

> Throughout this epistle, the writer emphasized the impor-
> tance of the *future hope*. His readers were prone to *look back*
> and want to *go back*, but he encouraged them to follow
> Christ's example and *look ahead* by faith. The heroes of faith
> named in the previous chapter lived for the future, and this
> enabled them to endure (Heb. 11:10, 14–16, 24–27).
>
> —*Be Confident*, page 161

4. What are ways today's church looks backward instead of forward? How can Christians follow the example of the heroes of faith and look ahead to the joy that awaits us? What role does faith play in the ability to look ahead?

From Today's World

If you've spent any time at all in the gym or playing a sport, you're probably familiar with the "no pain, no gain" philosophy of exercise. While working out to the point of actual pain may be unwise and potentially unhealthy, the truth that it takes work to accomplish athletic goals is almost universally accepted. Especially in a culture where people try to take shortcuts through steroid use and other methods, the idea that healthy growth takes effort is worth underlining.

5. How does the message in Hebrews 12 speak to the "no pain, no gain" philosophy of training? What sorts of "hardship" will believers endure as they grow their faith?

From the Commentary

> As we run the Christian race, what is our goal? The writer
> explains the goal in Hebrews 12:14: *peace* with all men,
> and *holiness* before the Lord.
>
> —*Be Confident,* page 164

6. How does the writer of Hebrews explain how to reach the goal of peace
with all men and holiness before the Lord? Underline the key concepts for
this as written in Hebrews 12:14–19.

From the Commentary

> The *basis* for this fellowship is brotherly love. As Chris-
> tians, these Hebrew people no doubt had been rejected by
> their friends and families. But the deepest kind of fellow-
> ship is not based on race or family relationship; it is based
> on the spiritual life we have in Christ.
>
> —*Be Confident,* pages 171–72

7. What are some examples of today's believers being rejected by friends and family? What happens when a church or community is based on anything other than a love for Christ?

From the Commentary

> Contentment cannot come from material things, for they can never satisfy the heart. Only God can do that. "Watch out! Be on your guard against all kinds of greed; a man's life does not consist in the abundance of his possessions" (Luke 12:15 NIV). When we have God, we have all that we need.
>
> —*Be Confident*, page 174

8. What are some of the ways people seek contentment from material things? How is this like the temptation the Hebrew Christians had to go back to the old covenant? Practically speaking, how do we learn to trust that when we have God, we have all that we need? What does that look like in day-to-day living?

More to Consider: Have you ever experienced a church split or significant disagreement within a church? What prompted that situation? In what ways was the spiritual foundation of the church involved or not involved in the dispute or conflict? Based on this experience, what are some reasonable cautions for churches that are beginning to face similar turmoil?

From the Commentary

While it is true that each member of a local body has an important ministry to perform, it is also true that God has ordained spiritual leaders in the church. I have been privileged to preach in many churches in America, and I have noticed that where the people permit the pastors (elders) to lead, there is usually blessing and growth.

—*Be Confident*, page 177

9. What happens to a church where the leader isn't given the latitude to lead? What are the risks of giving too much deference to a leader? How does a church find the right balance between lay leadership and the role of the elders or pastors? What advice would the writer of Hebrews offer in this regard?

From the Commentary

> The readers of this epistle were looking for a way to continue as Christians while escaping the persecution that would come from unbelieving Jews. "It cannot be done," the writer states in so many words. "Jerusalem is doomed. Get out of the Jewish religious system and identify with the Savior who died for you." There can be no room for compromise.
>
> —*Be Confident,* page 179

10. What do you know about the situation of Christians in countries where Christianity is either outlawed or disdained? How can Christians discover confidence even in the midst of persecution? What role does a growing faith play in dealing with difficult situations?

Looking Inward

Take a moment to reflect on all that you've explored thus far in this study of Hebrews 12—13. Review your notes and answers and think about how each of these things matters in your life today.

Tips for Small Groups: To get the most out of this section, form pairs or trios and have group members take turns answering these questions. Be honest and as open as you can in this discussion, but most of all, be encouraging and supportive of others. Be sensitive to those who are going through particularly difficult times and don't press people to speak if they're uncomfortable doing so.

11. What events or circumstances in your life make it difficult for you to endure? How does the message in Hebrews 12 speak to you about that difficulty?

12. Think about when you've experienced the greatest growth as a believer. What role did hardship play in that growth? What does this teach you about the importance of endurance?

13. What are some of the ways you express what the author of Hebrews refers to as "brotherly love" toward others? How does that love play out in church? In your family? At work? When among strangers?

Going Forward

14. Think of one or two things that you have learned that you'd like to work on in the coming week. Remember that this is all about quality, not quantity. It's better to work on one specific area of life and do it well than to work on many and do poorly (or to be so overwhelmed that you simply don't try).

Do you need to develop a greater endurance for difficult times? Act more lovingly toward others? Be specific. Go back through Hebrews 12—13 and put a star next to the phrase or verse that is most encouraging to you. Consider memorizing this verse.

Real-Life Application Ideas: Think about how content you feel in your life today. How much of that contentment comes from material things or the lack of them? What would it take to put your trust in God more than "stuff"? Consider making some lifestyle changes that will help put your focus back on being confident in God's role for you. What are those practical things you can do that will cause you to grow more in faith? Do them!

Seeking Help

15. Write a prayer below (or simply pray one in silence), inviting God to work on your mind and heart in those areas you've previously noted. Be honest about your desires and fears.

Notes for Small Groups:

- *Look for ways to put into practice the things you wrote in the Going Forward section. Talk with other group members about your ideas and commit to being accountable to one another.*

- *During the coming week, ask the Holy Spirit to continue to reveal truth to you from what you've read and studied.*

Summary and Review

Notes for Small Groups: This session is a summary and review of this book. Because of that, it is shorter than the previous lessons. If you are using this in a small-group setting, consider combining this lesson with a time of fellowship or a shared meal.

Before you begin ...
- *Pray for the Holy Spirit to reveal truth and wisdom as you go through this lesson.*
- *Briefly review the notes you made in the previous sessions. You will refer back to previous sections throughout this bonus lesson.*

Looking Back

1. Over the past ten lessons, you've examined the epistle to the Hebrews. What expectations did you bring to this study? In what ways were those expectations met?

2. What is the most significant personal discovery you've made from this study?

3. What surprised you most about the Hebrews author's arguments for finding your confidence in God? What, if anything, troubled you?

Progress Report

4. Take a few moments to review the Going Forward sections of the previous lessons. How would you rate your progress for each of the things you chose to work on? What adjustments, if any, do you need to make to continue on the path toward spiritual maturity?

5. In what ways have you grown closer to Christ during this study? Take a moment to celebrate those things. Then think of areas where you feel you still need to grow and note those here. Make plans to revisit this study in a few weeks to review your growing faith.

Things to Pray About

6. Hebrews is packed with theology and some difficult-to-understand concepts. As you reflect on these words, ask God to reveal to you those truths that you most need to hear. Revisit the book often and seek the Holy Spirit's guidance to gain a better understanding of what it means to be confident in God.

7. Hebrews focuses primarily on the subject of the new covenant and Jesus' superior sacrifice. These themes were of particular importance to the intended audience for the letter, but they also have huge significance for

138 \ The Wiersbe Bible Study Series: Hebrews

believers today. Another big theme in Hebrews is that of faith. Spend time praying for each of these topics.

8. Whether you've been studying this in a small group or on your own, there are many other Christians working through the very same issues you discovered when examining Hebrews. Take time to pray for each of them, that God would reveal truth, that the Holy Spirit would guide you, and that each person might grow in spiritual maturity according to God's will.

A Blessing of Encouragement

Studying the Bible is one of the best ways to learn how to be more like Christ. Thanks for taking this step. In closing, let this blessing precede you and follow you into the next week while you continue to marinate in God's Word:

May God light your path to greater understanding as you review the truths found in the book of Hebrews and consider how they can help you grow closer to Christ.

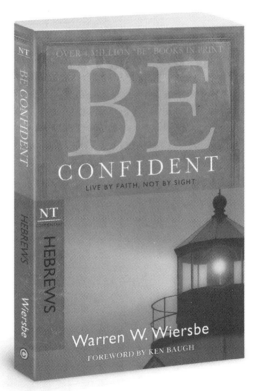

The "BE" series . . .

For years pastors and lay leaders have embraced Warren W. Wiersbe's very accessible commentary of the Bible through the individual "BE" series. Through the work of David C. Cook Global Mission, the "BE" series is part of a library of books made available to indigenous Christian workers. These are men and women who are called by God to grow the kingdom through their work with the local church worldwide. Here are a few of their remarks as to how Dr. Wiersbe's writings have benefited their ministry.

"Most Christian books I see are priced too high for me . . .
I received a collection that included 12 Wiersbe
commentaries a few months ago and I have
read every one of them.
I use them for my personal devotions every day and they
are incredibly helpful for preparing sermons.
The contribution David C. Cook is making to the
church in India is amazing."

—Pastor E. M. Abraham, Hyderabad, India

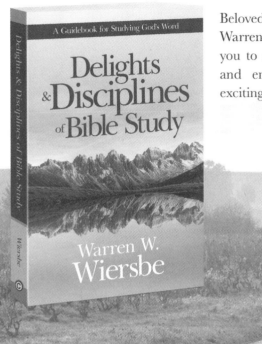